HOLIDAY JOKES & SWEET TREATS

# HALLOWEEN TRICKS & TREATS

**Anna Anderhagen**

**Consulting Editor, Diane Craig, MA/Reading Specialist**

Super Sandcastle

An Imprint of Abdo Publishing
abdobooks.com

**abdobooks.com**

Published by Abdo Publishing, a division of ABDO, PO Box 398166, Minneapolis, Minnesota 55439. 

Printed in the United States of America, North Mankato, Minnesota
102024
012025

Design: Layne Halvorsen, Mighty Media, Inc.
Production: Mighty Media, Inc.
Editor: Liz Salzmann
Cover Photographs: Mighty Media, Inc. (recipe photos); Shutterstock Images
Interior Photographs: Adobe Stock, pp. 6 (truck), 12 (hands), 13 (containers, washing plate), 22 (skull); Layne Halvorsen/Mighty Media, Inc., p. 4 (bats), Mighty Media, Inc. (recipe photos), pp. 10, 14, 15, 16, 17, 18, 19, 20, 21, 22, 23, 24, 25, 26, 27, 29; Shutterstock Images, pp. 1 (rolling pin), 4 (child), 5 (children), 6 (mummy), 7 (child), 8 (all), 8–9 (sprinkles), 9 (all), 11 (all), 14 (bats), 16 (witch hat, broom), 20 (goblin), 24 (green hand), 28 (bats), 28–29 (child), 29 (rolling pin, plate), 30 (child, ice cream), 31 (child)
Design Elements: Shutterstock Images (abstract doodles, kitchen utensil doodles)

Library of Congress Control Number: 2024938369

**Publisher's Cataloging-in-Publication Data**
Names: Anderhagen, Anna, author.
Title: Halloween tricks & treats / by Anna Anderhagen
Description: Minneapolis, Minnesota : ABDO Publishing, 2025 I Series: Holiday jokes & sweet treats I Includes online resources and index.
Identifiers: ISBN 9781098295196 (lib. bdg.) I ISBN 9798384915249 (ebook)
Subjects: LCSH: Jokes--Juvenile literature. I Halloween--Juvenile literature. I Holidays--Juvenile literature. I Snack foods--Juvenile literature. I Cooking--Juvenile literature. I Halloween cookery--Juvenile literature.
Classification: DDC 398.7--dc23

## TO ADULT HELPERS

The sweet treats in this series are fun and simple. There are just a few things to remember to keep kids safe. Creating some treats requires the use of hot objects. Also, kids may be using messy materials, such as food coloring. Make sure they protect their clothes and work surfaces. Review the projects before starting and be ready to assist when necessary.

Super Sandcastle™ books are created by a team of professional educators, reading specialists, and content developers around five essential components—phonemic awareness, phonics, vocabulary, text comprehension, and fluency—to assist young readers as they develop reading skills and strategies and increase their general knowledge. All books are written, reviewed, and leveled for guided reading and early reading intervention programs for use in shared, guided, and independent reading and writing activities to support a balanced approach to literacy instruction.

# Contents


Halloween . . . . . . . . . . . . . . . . . . . . . . 4

Holiday Hoots! . . . . . . . . . . . . . . . . . . 6

Sweet Materials . . . . . . . . . . . . . . . 8

Melting Tips & Tricks . . . . . . . . . 10

Treats Prep . . . . . . . . . . . . . . . . . . . 12

Spooky Cookie Bats . . . . . . . . . . 14

Witch's Hats & Broomsticks . . 16

Ogre Boo!-gers . . . . . . . . . . . . . . . 20

Skeleton Bubble Baths . . . . . . . . 22

Witch Fingers . . . . . . . . . . . . . . . . 24

Keep Creating! . . . . . . . . . . . . . . . 28

Last Laughs . . . . . . . . . . . . . . . . . 30

Glossary . . . . . . . . . . . . . . . . . . . . 32

# HALLOWEEN

Halloween **traditions** started more than 2,000 years ago. Ancient **Celts** who lived mainly in Ireland, the United Kingdom, and France **celebrated** a **festival** called Samhain. This marked the end of summer and the beginning of winter.

In the 700s, the Christian church moved the Christian holiday All Saints' Day closer to Samhain. The night before All Saints' Day was known as All Hallows' Eve. Over time, the holidays merged.

When Irish, Scottish, and English **immigrants** came to the US, they brought these **traditions** with them. The holiday **eventually** became known as Halloween.

*What is a monster's favorite game?*

**Hide and shriek.**

# Holiday Hoots!

What is a mummy's favorite kind of music?

**Wrap.**

Why was all the food gone at the end of the Halloween party?

**Everyone was a-goblin.**

When do zombies stop trick-or-treating?

**When they are dead tired.**

What kind of car does Frankenstein drive on Halloween night?

**A monster truck.**

Why didn't anyone want to go trick-or-treating with Dracula?
Because he is a pain in the neck.
How do you know if a mummy catches a cold?
It starts coffin.
Why didn't the zombie go to school?
It felt rotten.
Why don't monsters eat clowns?
They taste funny.

# Sweet Materials

**Here are some of the ingredients and tools you will need to make the treats in this book.**

## Ingredients

- almond slices
- baking soda
- black gel food coloring
- bright green candy melts
- butter
- candy eyes
- chocolate almond bark
- chocolate-covered mint cookies
- cocoa powder
- cream-filled chocolate sandwich cookies
- food coloring
- Hershey's Kisses
- icing gel
- large pretzel rods
- light corn syrup
- milk
- mini chocolate chips
- mini marshmallows
- mini peanut butter cups
- plain popped popcorn
- premade peanut butter cookie dough
- pretzel sticks
- regular marshmallows
- salt
- soft caramel squares
- sprinkles
- sugar
- vanilla extract
- yogurt-covered pretzels

*What are a vampire's favorite fruits?*

**Neck-tarines and blood oranges.**

## Tools

- aluminum foil
- baking pan
- baking sheet
- bowls
- food-safe paintbrush
- fork
- measuring cups & spoons
- microwave-safe bowl
- mugs
- parchment paper
- plastic gloves
- saucepan
- scissors
- sealable plastic bag
- spoon
- toothpicks
- whisk
- wooden lollipop sticks

What do ghosts eat for dinner?

**Spook-etti!**

# Melting Tips & Tricks

Some of the recipes in this book require you to melt ingredients in the microwave. To melt means to heat something until it is soft or liquid. Here are some tips for melting success!

## General Tips

- Put the ingredient in a microwave-safe bowl.
- Microwave for 20 seconds at a time.
- Stir after each time. If you don't, the ingredient could burn.
- Repeat until the ingredient becomes creamy and smooth.

*Where do spiders do their Halloween shopping?*

**On the web.**

## Extra Tips for Caramel

- Use soft caramel squares, not hard caramel candies.
- Unwrap the caramels before microwaving them.

What do you call a ghost that gets too close to a bonfire?

**A toasty ghosty.**

## Extra Tip for Almond Bark

- Cut the almond bark into small **chunks**. Smaller chunks will melt more quickly.

## Extra Tips for Candy Melts

- Microwave the candy melts at 50 percent power for 30 seconds at a time.
- Stir them after every time, even if they don't look melted.
- If the candy melts get too hot, they become clumpy. Let the bowl sit for a few minutes to cool off. Then stir again.
- If you find that the candy melts are too still too thick and clumpy, stir in a spoonful of coconut oil or shortening.

# Treats Prep

## Be Safe

- Ask an adult for permission to use kitchen tools and ingredients.
- Ask an adult to help you use the microwave.
- Ask an adult for help when handling sharp or hot objects.
- Clean up spills right away.

## Get Ready!

- Wash your hands.
- Clean your work surface before you start.
- Read the list of tools and ingredients for the sweet treat you are making. Set out everything you will need.
- Read the whole recipe at least once before you start.

*What do you call a skeleton that is cleaning up?*

**The grim sweeper.**

## When You Are Finished

- Let hot treats cool completely.
- Put all the ingredients and tools away.
- Store leftover ingredients to use later.
- Wash all the dishes and cooking tools.
- Clean your work surface.
- Wash your hands before you eat your sweet treats!

# Spooky Cookie Bats

Why did the vampire need mouthwash?

**He had bat breath.**

## Ingredients

- 12 mini peanut butter cups
- 6 cream-filled chocolate sandwich cookies
- 2-ounce square of chocolate almond bark
- candy eyes

## Tools

- knife & cutting board
- microwave-safe bowl
- spoon

1. Unwrap the mini peanut butter cups.
2. Twist apart the chocolate sandwich cookies. Break the cookies in half.
3. Follow the tips on pages 10 and 11 to melt the almond bark.
4. Put a little melted almond bark on top of each peanut butter cup.
5. Press two cookie halves into the almond bark on each peanut butter cup. Arrange them so they look like bat wings.

6. Put a little melted almond bark on each bat.
7. Carefully press candy eyes into the almond bark on each bat. Let the almond bark set for about 10 minutes before serving.

*What is a vampire's favorite Halloween candy?*

**A sucker.**

# Witch's Hats & Broomsticks

What do witches study in school?

**Spelling.**

## Hats Ingredients

- 12 Hershey's Kisses
- 2-ounce square of chocolate almond bark
- 12 chocolate-covered mint cookies
- icing gel
- sprinkles

## Broomsticks Ingredients

- premade peanut butter cookie dough
- pretzel sticks
- 2-ounce square of chocolate almond bark
- 6 soft caramel squares

## Tools

- knife & cutting board
- microwave-safe bowls
- spoon
- baking sheet
- parchment paper
- measuring spoons
- fork
- sealable plastic bag
- scissors

## How to make the hats

1. Unwrap the Hershey's Kisses.
2. Follow the tips on pages 10 and 11 to melt the almond bark.
3. Dip the bottom of a Kiss into the melted almond bark. Place the Kiss in the center of a cookie. Repeat to put a Kiss on each cookie. Let them cool for 5 minutes.
4. Trace around each Kiss with icing gel. Pour sprinkles onto the gel.

*How do witches tell time?*

**With witch watches.**

## How to make the broomsticks

1. Line the baking sheet with parchment paper.
2. Put a tablespoon of cookie dough on the baking sheet. Shape it into a triangle. Repeat to make more cookie dough triangles.

Continued on the next page. 

3. Place the end of a pretzel stick under one point of each triangle. Press down on each cookie dough triangle with a fork to create bristle lines.

4. Follow the cookie dough package instructions to bake the cookies. Let them cool for at least 10 minutes.

5. Follow the tips on pages 10 and 11 to melt the almond bark.

6. Put almond bark on each cookie where the cookie meets the pretzel stick.

7. Follow the tips on pages 10 and 11 to melt the caramel squares.

8. Put the melted caramel in a plastic bag. Cut off the tip of one corner of the bag. **Squeeze** the bag to **drizzle** caramel onto the almond bark.

9. Put the cookies in the refrigerator for at least 10 minutes before serving.

What is it like to ride a witch's broom?

**It's terror-flying!**

# BREWTIFUL

# Ogre Boo!-gers

What do ogres wear to go trick-or-treating?

**Mas-scare-a.**

## Ingredients

- 10 cups plain popped popcorn
- 1 cup sugar
- ½ cup butter
- ¼ cup light corn syrup
- 20 drops yellow food coloring
- 10 drops green food coloring
- ¾ teaspoon baking soda

## Tools

- measuring cups & spoons
- large bowl
- saucepan
- spoon
- baking pan
- aluminum foil

YUM!

1. Preheat the oven to 200 degrees Fahrenheit (93°C). Put the popcorn in a large bowl.
2. Stir the sugar, butter, and corn syrup together in a saucepan. Bring the mixture to a boil over medium heat.
3. Stir in the food coloring and baking soda. The mixture will foam up a bit.
4. Pour the mixture over the popcorn. Toss to coat evenly.
5. Line the baking pan with foil. Spread the popcorn evenly in it.
6. Bake for 1 hour, stirring every 15 minutes. Cool completely before serving.

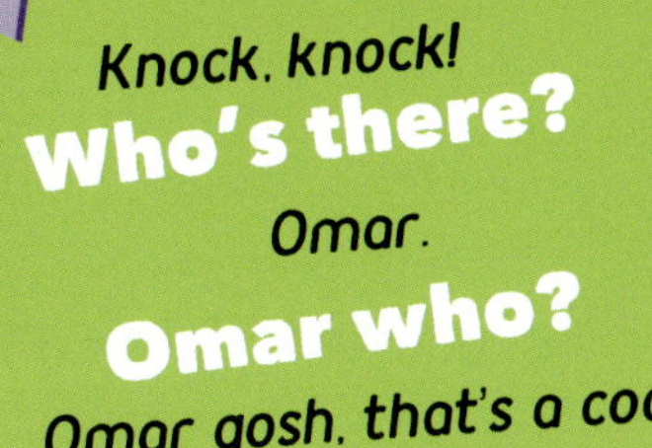

# Skeleton Bubble Baths

Why didn't the skeleton go to see a scary movie?

**It didn't have the guts.**

## Ingredients

- 3 regular marshmallows
- 6 mini chocolate chips
- 2 cups mini marshmallows
- 9 yogurt-covered pretzels
- 2 cups milk
- 4 tablespoons cocoa powder
- pinch of salt
- 3 tablespoons sugar
- ¼ teaspoon vanilla extract

## Tools

- 3 wooden lollipop sticks
- toothpick
- measuring cups & spoons
- saucepan
- whisk
- 3 mugs

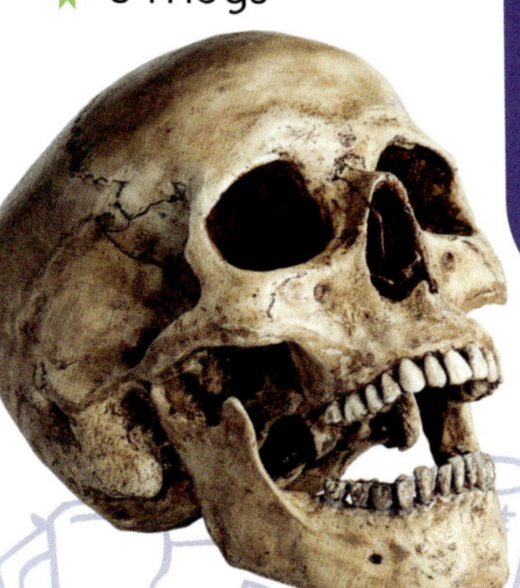

SPOOKY

1. Push a lollipop stick into the curved side of each regular marshmallow. Use a toothpick to make eye **sockets** in one flat end of each marshmallow. Push a chocolate chip point first into each socket.

2. Push a mini marshmallow up each stick. Add a pretzel. Repeat until each skeleton has three pretzels separated by mini marshmallows. Add a mini marshmallow below the last pretzel on each skeleton. These are the skeletons' ribs.

3. To make hot chocolate, whisk the milk, cocoa powder, salt, and sugar together in a saucepan over medium heat. Continue to heat the hot chocolate, whisking occasionally. Add the vanilla when the hot chocolate starts boiling. Then remove the pan from the heat.

4. Pour the hot chocolate into mugs. Place a skeleton in each mug. Serve with extra mini marshmallows.

*Why didn't the skeleton dance at the Halloween party?*

**It had no body to dance with.**

# Witch Fingers

What do you call two witches living together?
**Broom-mates.**

## Ingredients

- 12 large pretzel rods
- 24 almond slices
- black gel food coloring
- 12 ounces bright green candy melts

## Tools

- baking sheet
- parchment paper
- food-safe paintbrush
- microwave-safe bowl
- spoon
- toothpick

CREEPY

1. Line the baking sheet with parchment paper. Break the pretzel rods in half.
2. Use a food-safe paintbrush to paint one side of each almond slice with black gel food coloring. Set the almonds on the baking sheet to dry.
3. Follow the tips on pages 10 and 11 to melt the candy melts.
4. Hold the unbroken end of a pretzel and coat it almost entirely with melted candy. This is a finger.

Knock, knock!

**Who's there?**

Diane.

**Diane who?**

I'm Diane to eat my Halloween candy.

Continued on the next page. 

5. Press a painted almond to the pretzel near the coated end. This is the fingernail. Set the finger on the baking sheet.
6. Repeat steps 4 and 5 with the remaining pretzel halves.

7. Before the fingers dry completely, use a toothpick to create wrinkles for the knuckles. Refrigerate the fingers for 10 minutes before serving.

What do you call a witch who lives on the beach?
A sand-witch.
WOW!

# Keep Creating!

You've made some **delicious** treats with the recipes in this book! Hopefully you had some laughs with your friends too. But could you make any of the recipes differently? Could you use different ingredients? Or can you think of your own spooky Halloween treat?

*What do vampires do with their friends?*

**They fang out.**

Do you or a friend have a nut **allergy**? Try making the Witch's Broomsticks with sugar cookie dough instead of peanut butter cookie dough. Use Rolo caramel candies instead of peanut butter cups for the Spooky Cookie Bats. Make the Witch Fingers with pumpkin seeds instead of almond slices for the fingernails.

Does a treat include an ingredient you don't like? Get creative! Find something else to use that you do like. For example, you could use Pocky sticks instead of pretzels for the Witch's Broomsticks.

Just use your imagination to keep creating!

# Last Laughs

What's a skeleton's favorite instrument?

**The trom-bone.**

What happened when the witch got in trouble at school?

**She was ex-spelled.**

What is a goblin's favorite dessert?

**Ice scream!**

Why was the mummy so tense?

**It was all wound up!**

Who did the zombie invite to its party?
Anyone it could dig up!
What does a ghost do to stay safe in a car?
It puts on the sheet belt.
Did you hear about the gloomy jack-o'-lantern?
It needed to lighten up.
What kind of rocks do ghosts collect?
Tombstones.

# Glossary

**allergy** – a sickness caused by touching, breathing, or eating certain things.

**celebrate** – to observe a holiday with special events.

**Celts** – people who lived about 2,000 years ago in many countries of western Europe.

**chunk** – a short, thick piece or lump of something.

**delicious** – very pleasing to taste.

**drizzle** – to pour in a thin stream.

**eventually** – in the end or at a later time.

**festival** – a celebration that often happens at the same time each year.

**immigrant** – someone who has left his or her home and settled in a new country.

**socket** – an opening that holds something, such as an eye.

**squeeze** – to press the sides of something together.

**tradition** – a belief or practice passed through a family or group of people.